Prayer Secrets

Prayer Secrets

Kenneth E. Hagin

Unless otherwise indicated, all Scripture quotations in this volume are from the *King James Version* of the Bible.

Second Edition
Seventeenth Printing 2003

ISBN 0-89276-005-2

In the U.S. write:
Kenneth Hagin Ministries
P.O. Box 50126
Tulsa, OK 74150-0126

In Canada write:
Kenneth Hagin Ministries
P.O. Box 335, Station D,
Etobicoke (Toronto), Ontario
Canada, M9A 4X3

1-888-28-FAITH
www.rhema.org

Contents

Chapter 1
The Prayer Secret of Praying According to God's Word

Jesus is our Mediator, Intercessor, Advocate, and our Lord. He stands between us and the Father. In no place in the Bible is it recorded that Jesus told His disciples to pray to Him. They were always to pray to the Father in His Name.

If we wish to be sure of reaching the throne, we must come according to the rules laid down in the Word of God.

JOHN 16:23,24
23 And in that day ye shall ask me nothing. Verily, verily, I say unto you, Whatsoever ye shall ask the Father in my name, he will give it you.
24 Hitherto have ye asked nothing in my name: ask, and ye shall receive, that your joy may be full.

Notice that Jesus said, "*. . . in that day ye shall ask me nothing.*" Jesus said this just before He went away. He was talking about the mediatorial session at the right hand of the Father when He ascended and was seated. Another translation reads, "In that day ye shall not pray to me." Jesus said to ask the Father in His Name. There is no other way to pray.

We can tell Jesus how much we love Him and appreciate Him, but when it comes to praying and asking, we must ask the Father through the Lord Jesus. Ephesians 3:14 and 15 says, "*For this cause I bow my knees unto the Father of our Lord Jesus Christ, Of whom the whole family in heaven and earth is named.*" It is not important what church you belong to, but it is important whose family you belong to.

Many people know about praying to God, but they know nothing about praying to the Father. They don't sound as if they really know Him. He is God to the world, but Father to me.

There is real joy in knowing that the Father will answer our prayers.

Smith Wigglesworth was installing some plumbing in a large house one day and the lady of the family came in, watched awhile, and then left. Finally, the woman came back into the room and locked the door. She asked Wigglesworth if he would tell her something. She asked, "What in the world is it that causes that wonderful expression on your face? You look as if you are full of joy."

He then told her that at breakfast that morning, his wife had come downstairs and informed him that two of their children were very ill. He said that before they even ate, they went upstairs, laid hands on their children, and they were instantly healed. Wigglesworth was just so happy because he had asked and had received. His joy was full.

The lady then asked Wigglesworth if she could know God like that. Standing right there, she accepted the Lord as her Savior. She then asked Wigglesworth if she could keep this experience, and he told her that the only way to keep it was to give it away. He told her to tell all her friends about being saved.

You see, Wigglesworth would have looked worried and sad if his children had still been ill. Instead, he had joy on his face. I believe it ought to be that way with all Christians. *". . . ask, and ye shall receive, that your joy may be full"* (John 16:24). You have to maintain that joy even before the manifestation comes.

Another time Wigglesworth was facing desperate financial need. He was visiting in the home of a very wealthy man but said nothing about his problem. He had to cast every care on the Lord and was whistling and very happy. The rich man was not in good spirits and he told Wigglesworth that he would give all he owned to have the spirit that Wigglesworth had. Wigglesworth told him that it wouldn't cost him anything; all he had to do was cast all of his cares on Jesus.

Some years ago, I was preaching in a church close to home. After I had been there about a week, the pastor asked me to stay on and preach longer. He asked me what salary I needed. I told him, and he replied that that was more than his church had ever paid an evangelist, but they would give me that amount. We then agreed that my needs would be supplied.

On Saturday, before the service on Sunday night, I went home and while I was there, I discovered that some emergencies had arisen and I needed several hundred dollars more. I knew when I went back to preach on Sunday that the pastor would be dismayed. I had already obligated myself to stay with him for a couple of weeks; therefore, all I could do was pray that the Lord would work out everything.

When I returned to the meeting, I did not say anything to the pastor. He told me later that they had not met the budget and that they did not have enough to pay the minimum he had promised me. Then I told him the amount I would need to have in order to meet my emergencies. About that time he became upset. I told him I would believe for it, and he could agree with me.

Later on, his wife told me she noticed that this financial trouble never bothered me a bit and that I seemed to be just as full of joy as ever. When the meeting was over, I had the money! Praise God! You see, the need was there, and God met the need. He gave me even more than I needed because I had walked by faith and not by sight.

Ephesians 5:20 says, *"Giving thanks always for all things unto God and the Father in the name of our Lord Jesus Christ."* Paul is telling us that it is to the Father and not to Jesus that we give thanks. The Name of Jesus is the access to the heart of the Father. When you desire to get an answer, follow the teachings of the Word. Pray to the Father in the Name of Jesus.

If you go to the bank with a check and ask the cashier to cash that check for a friend, you will be asked if you have money on deposit to guarantee it.

However, if that check has the name of a person who has an account at that particular bank, there will be no questions asked. We fail in our praying sometimes because our approach is all wrong. Thank God, Jesus has a standing in Heaven. He is the only approach to the Father. Let us use the mighty Name of Jesus that He has given us. He gave us the power of attorney to use His Name. He said, "*. . . In my name shall they* [believers] *cast out devils . . .*" (Mark 16:17). We have a right to use that Name against the devil. We have the right to use that Name to call out demons that bind men's souls.

Several years ago I was holding a meeting in east Texas, and we were studying the subject of prayer. In those meetings, two things took place that changed the whole course of my life. I had always believed in divine healing, but there were some cases of which I was afraid. In particular, these were mental cases or cases of demon possession. Then the Lord brought this comparison to me. It was as if a person were going to his car to unlock the door. He could say that he had unlocked the door, but really *he* didn't unlock it, because the key actually does the unlocking. When he starts the car, a key really does the work. A key starts the ignition. The key is the important factor in the whole situation.

I began to look at it from this standpoint: I am not going to cast out any devils. But Jesus gave me the key to do it. Jesus is the key to doing it. My fear of casting out devils ceased.

Secondly, as I studied the Word of God, I began to see something else. Let me encourage you to follow up on the Word after you read it and meditate upon it. Our spirits need to be educated and trained. Just because you read the Word of God is no sign that your spirit is educated. I could sit down and read a great deal of scientific material, but that is no sign I know what I am reading. You can read the Bible and not understand what you are reading. God's Word has to get down inside of you until you get the revelation of it in your heart.

Years ago, I read Einstein's theory of relativity and did not understand a thing I was reading. When I finished, I knew less than when I started. It confused me.

I think many times when people read the Word, they do not know what they are reading. They are trying to grasp it with their mentality. You must get the revelation of the Word in your heart.

As I read the scriptures, I began to meditate on them. I began to see something that I had never seen before. I saw that the devil is the author of all that is evil and that he is the god of this world. Satan has blinded and bound men.

I began to see that those of my own family who were unsaved were bound by the devil. No man would drive his automobile a hundred miles an hour and try to kill himself if he were in his right mind. But a fellow who is doped and drunk will, because he does not know what he is doing. No intelligent person will go through life wheeling and dealing and heading towards hell if he is in his right mind. For example, the Bible says when the prodigal son went home, "*. . . he came to himself . . .*" (Luke 15:17).

I received such a revelation of this that I was challenged. I had been praying for my oldest brother who had gone astray. But I discovered that all of my praying and fasting had been done in unbelief. (If you're expecting just prayer to do it, it won't work. This was revealed to me as I studied and meditated.)

I rose up with my Bible and said, "In the Name of the Lord Jesus Christ, you foul devil and demon of hell, and spirits that bind my brother's soul, I bind you, in the Name of the Lord Jesus Christ." I was full of joy, for I knew that it was just as good as done. I laid my Bible down and went out of the room whistling and singing.

About two weeks later as I was walking into my bedroom, I heard a voice say to me, "Oh, you don't think he'll really ever be saved, do you?" I stopped dead still, shutting that out of my mind and not even letting myself think about it. But way down inside, I was laughing. I told the devil that I had claimed his salvation, and that I knew it would come to pass. Two days afterwards at the very spot it had happened before, I heard that same voice again, asking the same question. Again I stopped and shut it out of my mind. I told the devil that I had claimed my brother's salvation and had broken Satan's power over him.

A few days later, I received a letter from my wife which stated that my brother had been saved. I wrote back and told her that I had known it for two or three weeks.

The Name of Jesus belongs to you too. That Name has authority on earth. You have a right to use that Name. If the devil can hold you in the thought arena, he will whip you. If you hold him in the arena of faith, he is the victim. Fight the good fight of faith. Peter said, "*. . . your adversary the devil, as a roaring lion, walketh about, seeking whom he may devour: Whom resist stedfast in the faith, knowing that the same afflictions are* *accomplished in your brethren that are in the world"* (1 Peter 5:8,9). You have to believe in your heart, your spirit, that what the Word says is true.

You see, the devil fought me twice. He tried to get me into the thought realm: "You don't think that your brother will ever be saved, do you?" That is what he kept saying to me. And that is exactly where many people try to solve their spiritual problems — with their minds. Then, they get all confused; they are worried sick, and have frowns on their faces.

But you need to act from your innermost being — from your heart — your spirit. Jesus said, "*. . . whosoever shall say . . . and shall not doubt in his heart, but shall believe that those things which he saith shall come to pass; he shall have whatsoever he saith"* (Mark 11:23).

I was preaching in Port Arthur, Texas, and the services were good, plus there were many healings. A Methodist woman came to the meetings and thanked me for the lessons we had been having. She told me that she had been sick for twenty years and had not been able to do her work. She could not get up and fix breakfast for her husband. She was in her forties and had two grown daughters. The doctors had not been able to help her. She had been to different healing meetings, yet had failed to receive her healing. But in my meetings, she said that I had taught her how to receive her healing.

Some time later I received a letter from this same woman with an offering enclosed, for she said that she wanted to have a part in helping someone else as she had been helped. She said that she had not known the importance of the Word of God and the Name of Jesus. In the privacy of her own home she looked up the Scriptures, raised her Bible and said, "Satan, you who have bound my body for all these years, I break your power over my life and claim my deliverance and my healing." She added that for the first time in twenty years she was doing all her own housework. Six months had passed, and she was still healed. She said that she had the vigor and vitality of a teenager, and that she had not felt so good since she was sixteen.

Then she told me about her husband who had never been saved. He would not go to church with her, although he was a good husband. In the privacy of her home, this woman took the Bible and said, "In the Name of Jesus, I break the power of the devil over my husband and claim his salvation." She said that it worked like magic. Overnight, he became a new creature. She said they were the happiest they had ever been in their lifetime.

She told about her daughters who smoked and danced. She said that she lifted her hands to heaven again and broke the devil's power over them, claiming their salvation. Within ten days, they became new creatures. They were delivered from every habit that had bound them, and heaven became their home.

When we learn to pray in line with what the Word of God says, our prayers will be effective!

Chapter 2
The Prayer Secret of Asking the Father in Jesus' Name

And in that day ye shall ask me nothing. Verily, verily, I say unto you, Whatsoever ye shall ask the Father in my name, he will give it you.

Hitherto have ye asked nothing in my name: ask, and ye shall receive, that your joy may be full.

— John 16:23,24

Jesus said this just before He went to the Cross. He was referring to the day in which we now live — after He went to the Cross, ascended up on High, and was seated at the right hand of the Father. He is now our Mediator, our Intercessor, our Advocate, and our Lord. He stands between the Father and us. When He says, "In that day," He means the day of the New Covenant.

When Jesus was here on the earth, the disciples could ask Him: they could talk to Him personally in the flesh.

A minister friend of mine never gets answers when he prays. Prayer is a struggle for him; because he prays to Jesus. I pray to the Father in the Name of Jesus. I've prayed this way for more than sixty years, and I've gotten everything I've asked for. I usually get it immediately. However, in the case of money it sometimes takes a few days because it has to come through various channels.

If this friend of mine were to ask me to pray for his finances, then he and I would have to agree on it. But his will could block my will and faith, for we have authority over demons and evil spirits, but we don't have authority over human spirits. If we had authority over human spirits, then we could make everybody get saved.

In John G. Lakes' book, *Sermons on Dominion Over Demons, Disease, and Death*, he tells about praying for a man who had sugar diabetes. They knelt to pray, when suddenly Lake asked the man what this $5,000 was that kept coming up before him. The man answered that his brother and he had been in business and his brother had died. His sister-in-law wanted him to liquidate the business, and he did. But he had kept $5,000 out for himself because he felt he deserved it, though it was actually her money. He told Lake that he had more than $5,000 in the bank, whereupon Lake told him to write out a check for $5,000, and then he would pray for him. The man wrote the check, walked to the mailbox, and sent it to his sister-in-law. When he came back he was healed. Sometimes matters like this nullify the effects of prayer.

Someone may say that they believe John 16:23 and 24, *but* . . .

Don't say "but," because there's not a "but" in that verse. Somebody says they believe this scripture, *if* . . .

There is not an "if" in that verse, so don't say "if." Just take Jesus at His Word.

Jesus says in John 16:24, *"Hitherto have ye asked nothing in my name . . . ."* Up to this time, no one had ever asked anything in His Name because He was on the earth. Praying in Jesus' Name didn't do any good until He began His mediatorial intercession at the right hand of the Father.

". . . Ask, and ye shall receive, that your joy may be full" (v. 24). Your joy cannot be full with your needs unmet. Your joy cannot be full if you cannot pay your rent or your bills. You cannot be full of joy if your children are sick.

Once when we were holding a service, the phone rang about six o'clock in the evening. It was my mother-in-law, who was taking care of our children, and she said that my son, Ken, had the mumps. He had been sick all afternoon. So she put Ken on the phone, and he said that he had told his grandmother to call because he knew that I would pray to God and God would heal him. When Ken hung up the phone, we prayed. She told us later that he lay down and fell asleep. About forty-five minutes later, she woke him up, told him to get his pajamas on, and go to bed. He had no fever, the swelling was gone, and he was fine! From that time on he never did have the mumps. God does hear and answer prayer! Too much of the time people just make a little stab in the dark and call that praying. They just *hope* that something will work out.

Let us call attention to the difference between praying for Jesus' sake and praying in the Name of Jesus. When you go to God and ask Him to do something for Jesus' sake, you are asking that it be done to help Jesus, on your credit. That sounds foolish because Jesus does not need the help, and you don't have any credit to guarantee it, if He did. We need the help, and He has the credit! From now on, don't pray, "For Jesus' sake."

If I have a stomachache, and I am praying for healing, I don't want it to stop hurting for Jesus' sake, it is to help me. I am the one who is hurting, not Jesus. If I owe one hundred dollars and I am praying for it to come in the offering, I do that to help myself.

I know that God has helped us on a lower level when we did not know any better, but we ought to be able to grow in prayer. The Bible teaches us that there is a similarity between physical and spiritual growth. No one is born a fully grown human being. People are born babies, and they grow up. We ought to be able to improve upon our praying just as we improve upon things physically.

When I was a young boy, I used to pray, "Now I lay me down to sleep. . . ." But I do not pray that way anymore. When some were spiritual babies, they might have prayed certain ways and God met them, helped them, and it sufficed for that day, but God wants us to grow spiritually.

When you meet God on His level, it makes a big difference. He requires more of you as you grow. When light comes and teaching is given, God requires you to walk in that light.

"*. . . In my name . . . they shall speak with new tongues*" (Mark 16:17). Every believer ought to be speaking in tongues. You can do it in Jesus' Name.

"*. . . In my name . . . They shall take up serpents . . .*" (Mark 16:17, 18). That means that if you are accidentally bitten by a viper, you can shake it off and claim immunity in the Name of Jesus. For example, when Paul the Apostle was shipwrecked on an island, he picked up some sticks to build a fire, and a viper fastened onto his hand. The people thought he had done something terrible, for it looked as if judgment had come upon him. They expected him to fall dead. They watched him, but he did not get sick and did not fall dead. They thought he was a god.

In east Texas, a minister friend of mine and some friends of his were out fishing in one of the rivers, and a cottonmouth moccasin bit him. It frightened the other men because they were not saved. My friend shook it off in the Name of Jesus and went about his business. His friends watched him, and saw that it never had any evil effect on him. This is not extreme because it is biblical.

The Bible says, "*. . . if they drink any deadly thing* [poison], *it shall not hurt them . . .*" (Mark 16:18). This means that if you accidentally take poison, you have the right to claim immunity in the Name of Jesus.

Some years ago, the superintendent of the Assemblies of God in the Texas district related this story to a group of ministers: Many years ago, the Texas district had a convention in Corpus Christi, Texas. The ministers did not have a great deal of money to stay in good hotels, so they stayed at a third-rate hotel. The hotel didn't have any running water, but there was a pitcher of water in the room. After they had finished eating, some of them began to get sick. Finally, about twenty or thirty of them became desperately ill, so they began praying for one another. As they prayed, someone had a revelation that the water in the hotel was poisoned, so they told the rest of the group not to drink it anymore. Everybody was healed. Then they took the remaining water to a nearby naval station and had it tested. The examining officers told them that there was enough poison in that water to kill a regiment of men.

Someone had tried to play a cruel joke on these ministers because everyone knew that this group believed in miracles and healing. None of the party had to have medical aid! They had a right to claim immunity in the Name of Jesus because they had accidentally been poisoned. This is not extreme teaching, because it is in the Word. The Bible says, "*. . . they shall lay hands on the sick, and they shall recover*" (Mark 16:18).

Notice that Jesus said, "*. . . In my name . . . they shall speak with new* *tongues . . . they shall lay hands on the sick, and they shall recover"* (Mark 16:17,18). You lay hands on people in His Name. You do the speaking in tongues, and the Holy Spirit gives the utterance. You have a right to do that in the Name of Jesus.

This is just as strong and legal as it can be. The ordinary child of God has just as much right to use the Name of Jesus against the devil as a minister does.

Someone said to me that if he had enough faith he could do what this scripture says. Jesus never said a word about faith in this scripture. He said, *"He that BELIEVETH . . . In my name . . ."* (vv. 16,17). You already have faith. If you believe in the Name of Jesus, then use it. It is not struggling for faith; it is just boldly taking our rights, and using what belongs to us.

In the business world, you have a right to use what is yours. You don't think about having enough faith. That does not enter your mind. It is when that person who needs a healing acts upon what belongs to him, that he gets his healing.

Too much of the time folks do not believe as they should in divine healing. They are merely mentally assenting that these things are so. We have people sitting in the church, testifying that they know the Word of God is true, but they still don't get their healing. They are not acting in faith and using the Name of Jesus. When we act on the Word, it works. James said, ". . . *be ye doers of the word, and not hearers only* . . ." (James 1:22). It is just a matter of knowing what belongs to us and acting on it. It is taking your legal right. James goes on to say, "For if any be a hearer of the Word, and not a doer, he deceives himself" (James 1:23). The margin says that he "deludes himself." We have many self-deluded people.

Act as boldly as you would in the business world. The Name of Jesus belongs to me just as much as my hands and feet belong to me. I just go ahead and use them because they are mine. You will find that the devil will seek to confuse you. He will seek to withstand you. But the Name of Jesus is yours — so use it!

We have plenty of people who pray, but the results prove that their prayers are to no avail. If you do not get results to your praying, then you are a prayer failure. If you are not expecting results, then there is no need to pray. Pray to profit. Great businesses do business to profit. We must make a business of prayer.

The foundation of this great country is Christianity. The basis of Christianity is a living religion that's in touch with a living God who hears and answers prayer. We should pray for results. If we pray and results do not follow, then we should seek to find the trouble. The great things of Christianity are all supernatural. If there are no results, then it shows that we have the form without the power. All the things that God has, are offered to us — if only we pray. If we don't have them, then it is because we have not made our prayer connection. God is still in the same business.

Through the years I have gone to churches where not a single soul has been saved for years. Why don't we just get down to the basic principles and find out what is the matter? God is not untrue. Miracles can still happen.

In the early days of the Assemblies of God movement, there was a preacher by the name of I. J. Jamison. He was formerly a Presbyterian minister. In his testimony he told that he was lecturing in a western city as a Presbyterian, and there was a forest fire raging in the area. About ten o'clock in the morning, he was at the barbershop getting a shave when a fellow came in with a telegram, asking the people in a nearby tent meeting to pray for rain. The men in the barbershop all began talking about the tent meeting where there were people who believed in this kind of thing. But they were afraid to take the telegram over to the tent. So Mr. Jamison agreed to take it and he handed it to the minister. He said that the minister quieted everyone and read the request, whereupon everyone began praying. Afterward, they thanked God that there would be rain. The minister gave Jamison the telegram and told him to send one back saying that there would be rain by ten o'clock that night. It shocked him. Jamison went back to the barbershop and told the men what had happened. They all laughed about it and read the weather report which said there would not be any rain for at least four or five days.

Jamison went on to his lecture, and then went home to bed. His wife had washed some clothes and left them out on the line, so he teased her about bringing them in because it was going to rain. They laughed about it and then about 9:30 they fell off to sleep. Directly, they were awakened by thunder and lightning. It was raining!

This really made Jamison wonder. After his own lectures were over, he began attending the tent meeting. He would sit at the back and take notes on everything. He could not understand why he had not seen all these things before. He said he knew there was a woman in the church whose daughter was insane. He had heard that this woman and some of the people were going to meet at the asylum to try to cast a devil out of her daughter. The mother was taking a dozen women with her. Jamison asked if he could go along. He met them at the asylum, and the attendant said they could not go in because the girl was violent and might kill them. They were stopped before a padded cell, where there was a young woman inside who looked like an animal. She hissed and spit; her eyes were ablaze. All this time the attendant was telling them that they could not go inside the cell because if they did, he would lose his job. Nevertheless, he unlocked the door. The mother went in, and the dozen women fell on their knees and started praying. Jamison and the attendant stood back and watched.

The daughter stepped back and climbed halfway up the padded wall. She made a leap at her mother like an animal, and the mother sidestepped her. The girl fell and then started to get up. The mother held her down and said, "Come out of her, devil, in the Name of Jesus." Jamison stood there and watched spellbound. For ten minutes the mother said this over and over again. Suddenly, the daughter relaxed and asked her if it was she. She threw her arms around her mother's neck and hugged and kissed her.

I. J. Jamison witnessed it and said that he wanted the Holy Ghost. He said that he was a candidate for that kind of praying. The mother had believed, and she received what she wanted.

Chapter 3
The Prayer Secret of Praying for Results

> *And in that day ye shall ask me nothing. Verily, verily, I say unto you, Whatsoever ye shall ask the Father in my name, he will give it you.*
>
> *Hitherto have ye asked nothing in my name: ask, and ye shall receive, that your joy may be full.*
>
> — John 16:23,24

We are to pray in the Name of Jesus to the Father. We are to pray for results. If results do not follow, then our prayer life is a failure.

I remember reading about Dr. Charles Price. Someone had phoned him and asked him to come to the hospital. He ordinarily did not go because of a lack of time, but the person calling had been close to him in days past, so he agreed to go. The woman in the hospital had been converted under his ministry. When he arrived, he found that she was dying of cancer. The doctor came while he was there, so Dr. Price told the woman that he would go home and pray for her. The doctor told him that it would be just a short while before she would die, and he thought it would be a good idea to pray because it would soothe her nerves. But Dr. Price told him that he wasn't going to pray for her so that her nerves would be soothed. He said that he was going to pray that God would *heal* her! The doctor looked astonished. He knew that it just couldn't be so. But Dr. Price did pray for her, and she was healed! He was praying for results.

P. C. Nelson, who was a minister, was run over by an automobile and the doctors said that he would lose his limb, but he was healed. He then held healing meetings across the nation for different churches.

Nelson was holding a meeting in a Baptist church, and praying for the sick. The pastor of another Baptist church in Arkansas who had gone to seminary with Nelson, heard that he was holding these services. This man attended and was very much opposed. He talked about Nelson at home, and his family decided to go to the services. He took his family and his mother, who was living with them, to the service.

The next morning they were talking about the service at breakfast. The Baptist pastor didn't think it was right to pray for someone publicly, but his mother said that she wouldn't criticize Nelson. Finally, their youngest child who was about five years old spoke up. He said that the only difference he could see, was that when his daddy prayed for folks on Sunday morning, he said, "Lord, bless the sick," while not really expecting anything to happen. But that Nelson prayed as if he *expected* God to heal them right then. This caused the minister to start thinking, so he decided to cooperate with the meetings.

He also saw that he ought to pray for results. There is no use praying if you are not praying for results. God does hear and answer prayer. He wants to hear and answer your prayer; but He didn't put all these statements in the Bible about prayer just to fill up space. They are there for *our* benefit.

ISAIAH 43:25,26
25 I, even I, am he that blotteth out thy transgressions for mine own sake, and will not remember thy sins.
26 Put me in remembrance: let us plead together: declare thou, that thou mayest be justified.

Notice that God said, *"Put me in remembrance."* Those who have been mighty in prayer have always been those who reminded God of His promises and brought His Word before Him.

Charles Finney is probably the most outstanding exponent of prayer. He is known as the man who prayed down revivals. He had the greatest success, and his converts were the most consistent since the days of the Apostle Paul. It is common knowledge that eighty-five percent of his converts remained true to God. D. L. Moody was a great evangelist, but only about fifty percent of his converts remained faithful. We have had a mighty move over the past several years, but it is common knowledge that not more than fifty percent of the converts have remained true to the Lord. Finney had the greatest success numbers' wise as far as keeping the fruit of his labor, since the days of the Apostle Paul — whole cities were stirred.

For instance, I read in Finney's autobiography that in 1829 he went to the city of Rochester, New York, where he conducted a meeting and practically everyone in town was saved. All the grog shops closed down. (We now call them honky-tonks and beer joints.) There was not a place left in town where one could buy anything to drink. The only theater in town closed down. There was such a revival that when a circus came to town, only two people went to see it, so it had to close. Everyone was interested in God. The revival was on. The people were just not concerned about anything else.

I also read that Finney went to hold another meeting when he was a Presbyterian. He had been talking about fifteen minutes when the power of God fell on him. About four hundred people fell off their seats onto the floor, and it was a Presbyterian church! He didn't know what was happening, but he said that he found out later they had all been sinners and had just gotten saved when they fell under the power. Finney prayed for revival. He was a real man of prayer. He said that he had some experiences in prayer that indeed alarmed him. He added that he found himself saying to the Lord, "Lord, You don't think that we are *not* going to have a revival here, do You? You don't think that You could withhold Your blessings?" He found himself reminding the Lord what He had promised.

George Whitfield, another minister, came over from England and preached on the streets. He was speaking in the public square in Boston, Massachusetts. When he began to preach, folks climbed up into the trees so they could see because the crowd was so large. Whitfield told them to come down out of the trees, because when the power of God came they would fall out of the trees.

Smith Wigglesworth said that God delights in His children having the audacity of faith to say, "God, You have promised it, so now do it." You say that in faith. This agrees with what God says, for God said, *"Put me in remembrance."* They were putting Him in remembrance of what He said. If God wants us to put Him in remembrance, then let's do it. Isaiah 43:26 said it.

We are certainly facing great needs everywhere. People are dying for the need of Christ. The sick need healing. The weak need strength. What is your part? Are you in His will? Are you doing what He wants you to do? Is your life right with God? Does your heart condemn you? If so, get right with Him now. Thank God, that doesn't take very long.

Whatever you are praying about, stand your ground until victory is manifested. God wants to send you the answer. This is a spiritual warfare against the host of darkness. The Bible says so in Ephesians 6:12.

> **EPHESIANS 6:12**
> **12 For we wrestle not against flesh and blood, but against principalities, against powers, against the rulers of the darkness of this world, against spiritual wickedness in high places.**

Bow down before the Mighty One and persist in prayer even though the enemy might try to hinder you. We have weapons with which to fight the devil. Our weapons are the sword of the Spirit, which is the Word of God and the mighty Name of Jesus. The demons cannot stand these weapons. You can defeat the devil every single time. Pray to victory.

If you are praying for the sick, claim their deliverance in Jesus' Name. Jesus said, "*. . . In my name . . . they* [believers] *shall lay hands on the sick, and they shall recover*" (Mark 16:17,18). Lay your hands on them and claim their deliverance in the Name of Jesus. You have solid ground on which to stand.

If it is money you need, pray that it be loosened. This is because the money is here in this natural realm. God is not a counterfeiter. He is not going to make any money and rain it down from Heaven. God put all the silver and gold and cattle on a thousand hills here for you and me. He did not put it here for the devil and his crowd. He put it here and gave Adam dominion over all of it. Then Adam committed high treason and sold out to the devil; thus the devil became the god of this world. Adam was the god of this world and in that he had dominion over it but he sold out to the devil, so now the devil has the dominion (2 Cor. 4:4). But, thank God, Jesus came and defeated the devil. He gave us the right to use His Name.

At one time I was poverty-stricken and had my nose to the grindstone. Then I began to see something. The Lord told me never to pray for money. He said for me not to ask Him to give me money, for it was down here. He instructed me that in the Name of Jesus, I should command the money to come. Whatever I wanted or needed, I should claim it. He said that He wanted His children to have the best. In God's Word, He said that He wanted His children to eat the good of the land. His Word declares, *"If ye then, being evil, know how to give good gifts unto your children, how much more shall your Father which is in heaven give good things to them that ask him?"* (Matt. 7:11).

We need to realize the principles by which God works. God has given us the Name of Jesus. He said it wasn't He who was holding finances from me; it wasn't He who did not want my children to have the right kind of food to eat. If it were, He wouldn't be the right kind of a Father. He reminded me that any sinner could be a father who was concerned about his children, and that even an animal could be concerned about his offspring. He said that there never was an earthly parent who desired to do more for his children than He did. He said that the problem was that His children did not cooperate with Him. He told me to command the devil to take his hands off the finances.

If you pray to God to give you one hundred dollars, you are putting all the responsibility upon Him. But the responsibility is on our part because through Jesus Christ, deliverance has already been made for us.

I immediately began to do what God said. From that day to this, I never pray anymore about money. I just tell Satan to take his hands off my money. I always say that I claim so much money. I always say that angels are ministering spirits who are sent to minister to those who are heirs of salvation. "To minister" means *to wait on* or *to serve*. When you go to a restaurant, a waitress comes to serve or to minister to you.

This is the illustration the Lord gave me when I was praying in the Spirit. Actually, I had a vision and saw an angel. Jesus informed me that that was my angel. Jesus spoke to me about the time when He said in His Word: "Suffer the little children to come unto Me" (Matt. 19:14). Then He also said, "Their angel is ever before My Father's face" (Matt. 18:10). Jesus spoke this passage of Scripture when the disciples were rebuking the people for pressing around Him when He was tired. Jesus told me that just because I grew up, I did not lose my angel. The Lord told me to tell my ministering spirits, or angels, to go and cause the money to come. I have been doing that, and it has been working ever since then.

As we pray, we receive the answers we need. Prayer is the life of the church. I believe that we're only in the beginning of the prayer conquest. I feel that there is a great deal more that God is going to do in these last days. Learn the secret of praying for others. Pray for men and women by name. Don't just lump them together and pray for them as a group. Don't just pray for God to save souls. Mention their names specifically to God.

In the last church I pastored we had a unique prayer meeting. I told the people I wanted them to come on Thursday night and write on a piece of paper the name of the person they wanted most to see saved. If it were a husband and wife, they were to write both names down.

It turned out that the weather that night was very bad with a great deal of sleet and snow. Everyone was instructed to stay off the streets. We were not used to this kind of weather, neither did we have the equipment to handle it. Nevertheless, nineteen people came to the meeting.

I gathered up all the names, put them in the offering plate, and mixed them up. Then we passed the plate around, and each one took a name. I took one and said that I was going to pray for that particular person to be saved during the coming revival.

I told them to listen to what I said and then agree with it. I finished my prayer and we lifted our hands and praised God because that person was saved. I told the people not to pray for that person anymore, because we had already settled it. We went right down through the list and prayed for each one. All the people for whom we prayed except two, were saved during that meeting. I had never had that kind of success in my life.

Preaching at a camp meeting in 1954, I met a woman whose husband had been one of those we had prayed for. I'd heard that he had gotten saved.

You see, all those people we prayed for, except two, were saved within a month's time, and the other two were saved before the year was over.

When the meeting concluded, this couple came up, and the husband said, "Brother Hagin, I want to hug your neck; you know that I am your brother now." He said that he had gotten saved that year, after they moved back to California.

I was glad to know that prayer still works. When we pray for results according to God's Word, God's Word does not fail!

Chapter 4
The Prayer Secret of Agreeing and Praying In the Spirit

We are talking about prayer secrets. Here is the secret of agreeing.

MATTHEW 18:19
19 Again I say unto you, That if two of you shall agree on earth as touching any thing that they shall ask, it shall be done for them of my Father which is in heaven.

Do not put any limitations on that scripture. Let's just take God at His Word.

It is like the story we were told about a little girl. Her pastor kept saying, "That doesn't mean that," and "This doesn't mean this." She finally asked, "If Jesus did not mean what He said, then why didn't He say what He meant?" That is a pretty good thought.

If He didn't mean what He said, then why didn't He say what He meant? I believe Jesus said what He meant and meant what He said.

Several years ago at Christmastime I was preaching in west Texas. Although I had been there for three weeks the pastor wanted me to stay for three more weeks, and I still had another meeting before Christmas.

The pastor then informed me that he had a big payment every year on the church property, and each Sunday night in December he took an offering for this purpose. He said if I would stay, he would take up an offering for the payment first, and then take up my offering later.

He said he realized that I would need extra money at Christmastime since I would not be in meetings during the holidays, but he was not sure if his people could give any extra.

Nonetheless, I agreed to stay, believing that I would receive sufficient offerings.

I wrote my wife telling her that I was going to stay on, and that I wanted her to open her Bible the next Sunday afternoon to Matthew 18:19 and agree with me for so much money. I assured her that I would do the same. We claimed half again as much as we had been getting each week.

The next Sunday night the pastor took up his offering for the property and then mine. I received three dollars more than what my wife and I had agreed upon.

The next week I wrote my wife telling her to do the same thing again on the following Sunday afternoon, and that I would do likewise. When the week was over, we received one dollar and forty-nine cents above the amount we had asked for.

The Sunday night before Christmas, the church had a Christmas program, and I preached only fifteen minutes. Afterwards, the pastor took up an offering again for the property and then one for me.

After the service, we went to the parsonage, and the pastor asked me how much I had gotten for that week.

I told him that the deacons had not yet told me. Since the deacons were busy, the pastor and I counted the money. The offering was about twenty dollars short of what my wife and I had claimed. I suggested that we count it again, because the money had to be there. I told him what my wife and I had done, and I said that if it were not there, then I would have to go to every church where I had preached and tell them that Jesus was a liar and that the Bible was not so. If it did not work, I wanted to throw it away. I am just that honest.

I do not mean that things will come to you like ripe cherries falling from a tree, because you have to stand your ground. You have to stand your ground against the devil. In anything else in life, people will fight for their rights and what belongs to them. They will lose sleep and put forth every effort. But when it comes to spiritual things, they will roll over, shut their eyes, and play dead. We need to get down to business and find out where the answer is. God's Word works. Many times in prayer I have gone right over the same ground again and again.

If I had a very valuable ring and found that I had lost the setting out of the ring, I would go over the ground carefully where I thought I had lost it. I would get down on my hands and knees, crawling around, if necessary, looking for it. When it comes to spiritual matters I do the same thing — I retrace my steps.

So I told the pastor that the money had to be there. We counted it again and we were still short. He counted half the money, and I counted the other half. Then he counted the half that I had counted, and I counted his half. We still arrived at the same figure. I told him that it just had to be there. We decided to count it again. He said that we would count all night until we got it.

Suddenly, I remembered that the pastor's wife had bought a Bible from me before church. She had paid me for it and had put the seven dollars and fifty cents in an envelope. She told me at the same time that there was a personal offering that she did not want to go through the church. She told me not to tell even her husband about it. It was a twenty-five dollar offering, and I had forgotten all about it.

Then I told him that I had a twenty-five dollar offering, but I didn't tell him who gave it to me. Therefore, I had five dollars above what we had claimed!

Stand on God's Word and say that it has to be. Look the storm in the face like Paul did. Jesus' Word is more sure than the word of an angel. Paul said, "*For there stood by me this night the angel of God, whose I am, and whom I serve*" (Acts 27:23). He concluded saying, "*Wherefore, sirs . . . I believe God, that it shall be even as it was told me*" (Acts 27:25).

God's written Word is even more sure than the word of an angel. Look at the contradictory circumstances in the face and say, "Wherefore sirs, I believe God that it shall be even as it was told me." You will find out that the devil and demons will relent in their opposition, and the answer will come. Stand your ground and God will hear you. Look at the foreboding clouds in the face and say, "Wherefore sirs, I believe God that it shall be even as it was told me."

You will find out then that the devil and demons will relent in their opposition, and the answer will come. Stand your ground, and God will hear you.

In order for the prayer of agreement to work, there has to be two of you and you have to be on earth. That fits us. The strongest assertion that you can make in the English language is to say, "*I will* or *I shall*." You cannot make any stronger assertion than that. Jesus said, "*. . . it SHALL be done for them of my Father which is in heaven*" (Matt. 18:19).

In 1957, I was preaching in Salem, Oregon, during a recession that was occurring in the nation. Oregon was one of the states that felt the recession desperately. An unemployed mechanic from the church installed some new brakes on my car at his house. He had worked for a company for nineteen years as a mechanic, but the business had to close down.

After the meeting, this Christian mechanic and his wife and my wife and I were eating together, and they related what had happened to them after I preached on Mark 11:23, *"For verily I say unto you, That whosoever shall say unto this mountain, Be thou removed, and be thou cast into the sea; and shall not doubt in his heart, but shall believe that those things which he saith shall come to pass; he shall have whatsoever he saith."*

I had invited people in the meeting to come forward to speak in faith for whatever they wanted to see come to pass in their lives. That night as this man and woman were going home, the woman asked her husband what he had said. He then asked her the same question. They had some land which they had been trying to sell for several years; she told her husband that she had asked for the lot to be sold. He said that he had asked the very same thing.

The next morning at the breakfast table she told her husband to go back to the real estate agent and list the lot again. He went to the real estate agent who told him that the property would not sell. The Christian mechanic told the real estate agent that he wanted to list it anyway. The agent agreed and suggested that he see a man who had tried to buy the lot before at a lower price. The Christian mechanic found the man and learned that he was still interested in the lot. The man would even buy it for the price that the couple had asked for.

For two years this couple had needed the extra money and could have had it, if they had only *said* it. Instead of believing with the heart they had been praying that *God* would do something about it. *We* have our part to play too.

This Christian mechanic also worked in the forests when weather permitted. The man who bought the lot of land owned a fleet of trucks, and he asked the mechanic if he would like to have a job. He accepted the job, which was year-round employment and the salary was one hundred dollars more than what he had been getting. His wife said that they had always known Mark 11:23 and 24 was in the Bible, but that this was the first time they had ever really acted on it.

It is a sad thing that Spirit-filled Christians go through life and never act upon the Word. God's Word is true. Jesus did not say that it *might* be done or that there was a possibility that it *could* be done. Instead, He said that it *shall* be done! If you agree on anything, it shall be done. Instead of arguing with the Bible, why don't you just side with it.

Years ago when I was a Baptist boy, a friend of mine worked for his brother in a little garage that had hardly enough room to get one car in it. It was during the Depression days. His brother paid him three dollars a week and fed him. In addition, both brothers tried to help their parents who were very poor.

I remember I stopped by to see my friend, and he was working on a '34 Chevrolet. His brother had just left. He told me that he wanted me to pray about something with him. He had been going with a young lady, and he wanted to get married, but he couldn't on three dollars a week. He wanted me to pray that he would get a good job, because he did not even have any dress pants. He said he had applied for a job, but the men who took his application told him that there were two thousand ahead of him. He was going to apply for another job at the cotton mill, and he wanted me to agree with him that he would get it. Even though there were hardly any jobs, he knew God would do something about it.

I told him about Matthew 18:19, and we agreed that he would have that job within ten days. On the tenth day they called him, and he went to work for ten dollars a week. In a little while he bought himself a couple of suits of clothes, and in about nine months he got married on ten dollars a week.

He stayed there until he was promoted to be one of the bosses, earning a good salary. Then God called him to preach, and he went into the ministry.

This was my first experience in acting upon this verse of Scripture. It will work because it is God's Word. You can be mighty in prayer alone, but you can be mightier with someone joining you.

I remember Smith Wigglesworth telling about an English Presbyterian lady who had gone to his mission and received the baptism of the Holy Spirit.

(You may have experienced that yourself when you first received, you thought everyone would be happy for you, but you found out later that maybe they were not so thrilled!)

This lady went back to her church and started speaking in tongues, whereupon they threw her out. Her husband was on the board, and they told him that he would have to put a stop to it, or else they would have to excommunicate her for good.

He went home angry and informed her that she would have to choose between the Holy Spirit and him. He would give her ten days to make up her mind. She sent word for Wigglesworth to come to pray for her.

When he came, he saw that her face and eyes were red from crying. She told him that he was too late. Nonetheless, Wigglesworth assured her that God never sent him anywhere too late. She related the story and added that it was the tenth day.

At the breakfast table that morning her husband had asked her what her decision was. She told him that she could not give up the Holy Spirit, so he packed and left. Wigglesworth told her that if they agreed in prayer, her husband would be back. She replied, "You don't know my husband!"

He answered, "No, I don't know him, but I know my Jesus." She informed him that her husband never went back on his word. After a little time Wigglesworth succeeded in showing her what the Word said. He told her that all they had to do was to agree on earth. Finally, she agreed to agree with Wigglesworth.

They prayed and asked that her husband would come back. While they were praying, she began praying in the Spirit. Wigglesworth told her that *when* her husband came back that night (he didn't say "if"), she should be very nice and act as if nothing had happened at all. He added that after her husband went to bed she should go to another room to be alone, start praying in the Spirit, and when she was in the Spirit, she should go quietly and lay her hand on him and claim his soul.

Wigglesworth left, and the woman's husband came back that evening. She cooked him his favorite supper and later when she was praying while he was asleep, she laid her hand on him and claimed his soul. The minute she touched him, he jumped out of bed and asked the Lord to save him. He then confessed that he was a board member of the church but was not really saved. He was converted, and a few minutes later he was also filled with the Spirit. This all happened because Wigglesworth and this woman had agreed in prayer.

> **ROMANS 8:26**
> **26 Likewise the Spirit also helpeth our infirmities: for we know not what we should pray for as we ought: but the Spirit itself** [Himself] **maketh intercession for us with groanings which cannot be uttered.**

Dr. P. C. Nelson affirms that the Greek translation says that the Spirit makes intercession, "with groanings which cannot be uttered in articulate speech." Articulate speech means your normal kind of speech. This verse includes praying with tongues. That agrees with what Paul says in First Corinthians 14:14: *"For if I pray in an unknown tongue, my spirit prayeth, but my understanding is unfruitful."* The Amplified Bible says, ". . . my spirit [by the Holy Spirit within me] prays . . . ."

We know not what to pray for as we ought. You cannot possibly know in your natural mind what to pray for as you ought. For instance, if I am praying for someone I know, and I ask God to bless him, all I am doing is salving my conscience so I can say that I prayed for him. You can just say what you want to, but we know not what to pray for as we ought. Thank God, the Spirit helpeth our infirmities.

That does not mean that this is something the Holy Spirit does apart from you. That would make the Holy Spirit responsible for your prayer life and He is not, because the Bible teaches that *you* are responsible. The Holy Spirit is not sent to do your praying for you, but He is sent to help you in every aspect of life, including your prayer life. These groanings come out of your spirit and escape your lips; that is the Spirit helping you. Some things come out that just cannot be expressed in words. These groanings are inspired by the Holy Spirit, and they come from within you. Often by praying this way, you are interceding.

The prayer of intercession is praying for another.

Charles Finney began his ministry as a Presbyterian and later on became a Congregationalist. He knew something about the Holy Spirit. He is known as the man who prayed down revivals. Finney was holding a revival meeting in a certain city. The wife of one of the leading doctors of the city was a wonderful Christian woman and leader, but the doctor himself was an infidel. He would make fun of his wife. She felt that Finney, who had been a lawyer, would be able to help her husband. She kept insisting that Finney come to her house on one of his days off. He agreed to come on Monday for a noon meal.

This doctor had a brother who was a farmer; he was a very religious man and had come to attend the meetings. This farmer brother was staying in the home with the doctor and his wife, so at the time appointed, Finney came and everyone was seated at the table. The lady asked Finney to pray; as he bowed his head, he was checked in his spirit and felt that the Lord wanted the farmer brother to pray. The brother began praying, when suddenly he took ahold of his stomach and started groaning. He then jumped up from the table and ran to his bedroom.

The doctor thought something was wrong with him physically, and jumped up to follow his brother. Finney followed. As Finney went into the room, the doctor was coming out to get his bag because he thought his brother had some kind of stomach cramps. Finney knew what the matter was. He stopped the doctor, informing him that there was nothing wrong with his brother. Finney told the doctor that his brother had the spirit of travail and intercession, and that he was praying for the doctor's lost soul. The doctor jerked loose from Finney and said that he did not believe it. The doctor left and Finney went into the room and kneeled down by the brother, and began to pray.

You can help lift a spiritual load just like you can a physical load.

Finney said that within a few minutes he could feel the burden coming off on him. For forty-five minutes they stayed there weeping and groaning.

When you do this, sometimes you feel as if your own soul is lost, but really it isn't. Because you are taking someone else's burden upon yourself, you actually feel on the inside of you, as if you are lost.

Some have had this spirit of groaning and did not know what it was. It is intercession for a lost soul. If the Spirit of God comes upon you and groanings start welling up from your inner man, go ahead and groan and pray it out. Although you do not take it upon yourself to just groan in the flesh, there is a groaning of the Spirit when the Holy Spirit takes hold with you in prayer.

Finney said that after they had prayed, they started laughing. You should always pray until you have a feeling of praise. He said they rejoiced and laughed for a while.

After Finney came downstairs, he knocked on the doctor's study door. He told him that he had a word for him from his brother. The doctor opened the door and asked him how his brother was. Finney told him that his brother had been praying for the doctor's lost soul. He added that they had prayed it through, and that he was just as good as saved. Finney said the doctor dropped his head and started crying. Then he fell down on his knees and was gloriously saved.

Yes, there is a prayer of intercession. Yes, there is a ministry of intercession. Do not be afraid to yield to it. Paul says, *"For if I pray in an unknown tongue, my spirit prayeth . . ."* (1 Cor. 14:14).

My spirit is not coming from my mind or my head. The Holy Spirit is helping me. I do not know exactly what to pray for as I ought. So I begin praying in the Spirit, and I often get a revelation of what I am to pray for. Whether or not you have a revelation, pray that way anyway because you know it is Bible and it is scriptural.

A young Texas minister was hit head-on by a drunk driver. When his father arrived at the hospital they told him that his son's neck was broken and that he was paralyzed from the waist down. Doctors gave him little hope of recovering.

The father went back the next night, and found him unconscious. He told the doctor that he was going to stay all night and pray. The father prayed in tongues, and at midnight he was still praying in tongues. He prayed altogether about ten hours in the spirit.

At six o'clock in the morning, he went to his son's bed and saw him lying there with his eyes open. The son assured him that he was all right because God healed him. He said he had feeling all over his body. The two began praising the Lord. The doctor came in, and the boy told him that God had healed him. He asked the doctor to remove the cast, but the doctor said no, because his neck and back were broken. After much persuasion, they x-rayed him and said that they could not even find where his bones had been broken. They kept him there for a day or two to check him, and finally told him that he could go home. He was miraculously healed and is still preaching the Gospel.

The father got the job done when he began to pray in the Spirit. He got the help of the Holy Spirit in praying. You can increase your power in prayer one hundred percent by praying in the spirit and in tongues.

A Sinner's Prayer To Receive Jesus as Savior

Dear Heavenly Father,

I come to You in the Name of Jesus.

Your Word says, "... *him that cometh to me I will in no wise cast out*" (John 6:37),

So I know You won't cast me out, but You take me in,

And I thank You for it.

You said in Your Word, "*Whosoever shall call upon the name of the Lord shall be saved*" (Rom. 10:13).

I am calling on Your name,

So I know You have saved me now.

You also said, "... *if thou shalt confess with thy mouth the Lord Jesus, and shalt believe in thine heart that God hath raised him from the dead, thou shalt be saved. For with the heart man believeth unto righteousness; and with the mouth confession is made unto salvation"* (Rom. 10:9,10).

I believe in my heart that Jesus Christ is the Son of God.

I believe that He was raised from the dead for my justification.

And I confess Him now as my Lord,

Because Your Word says, "*. . . with the heart man believeth unto righteousness . . .*" and I do believe with my heart,

I have now become the righteousness of God in Christ (2 Cor. 5:21),

And I am saved!

Thank You, Lord!

Signed ____________________________

Date ______________________________

About the Author

The ministry of Kenneth E. Hagin has spanned more than 65 years since God miraculously healed him of a deformed heart and an incurable blood disease at the age of 17. Today the scope of Kenneth Hagin Ministries is worldwide. The ministry's radio program, "Faith Seminar of the Air," is heard on more than 200 stations nationwide and on the Internet worldwide. Other outreaches include *The Word of Faith*, a free monthly magazine; crusades conducted throughout the nation; RHEMA Correspondence Bible School; RHEMA Bible Training Center; RHEMA Alumni Association; RHEMA Ministerial Association International; RHEMA Supportive Ministries Association; and a prison outreach.